TABLE OF CONTENTS

Day

1

Setting the Right Sales Mindset

Think of the worst sales person you can imagine. We've all had our experiences with them. They are pushy. They need a sale. They may be aggressive, perhaps even like the stereotypical used car salesman. In short, they are *nothing* you would ever want to be. Am I right?

Now, think about a sales person that you love. They helped you find just the right gift for a loved one. They took you around the store or the showroom. The conversation was light, even lively. Hey, this person could even be your friend one day.

Which version is what sales people are all about?

You decide.

If you go with door number 1, then you'll never be able to be a sales person or sell yourself. This is because you would *never* want to align yourself with something – dare to *be* – something you do not like. You cannot hate something and also try to become it. It just doesn't work.

On the other hand, you *can* choose to change your mind about what selling *is* and what it looks like. And, that's why we go to door number 2. That friendly person is also a sales person. That person who might be your friend one day could be just like you.

There's only one difference between door 1 and door 2.

That is…where the person's focus is.

Door 1's sales person is thinking about him or herself. She doesn't care about you or your needs. She is thinking she needs this sale. He is thinking about his quote. Your needs don't even enter the picture because there isn't enough room in this picture for anyone else's needs.

Door 2 is all about you. She smiles warmly at you as you enter the store. She wants to know what brings *you* in. She wants to hear about *your* vision for this gift. He asks what your wife's name is so you can bring her into the conversation. Suddenly, the conversation is a painting where you are thinking about giving this gift to your darling wife and the sales person is assisting you in creating your grand vision. The focus is all on *you*.

In your job hunting, which sales person are you?

If you chose Door number 1, don't despair. This is common. After all, you do have a mortgage or rent to pay, perhaps your 401(k) took a beating and it is getting down to go time on getting a job. Your unemployment may be running out. It's *natural* to think of your own needs.

Sales Pro Secret #1

Don't Think of Your Own Needs While You Are Selling

The time to think of your own needs is *before* you go to your interview or networking meetings (more on how to do this in Day 6). When you know ahead of time what you are looking for, then you can spend the rest of your time and energy focusing on *others* and their needs. The more you show up in service, the more likely you are to find yourself with others who are like you.

In this economy, as you can imagine, many people are focused on what *they* need, and this is not a feeling most people want to be around, so be alert for these people, and keep your mind focused on people who are *focused on others*. These are the *connectors*, the people who would be willing to help you connect to others or even a job.

Now, let's go back to Door 1 and Door 2. You definitely want to be the professional a future employer will find behind Door number 2. But, how do you do that?

First, you determine what kind of company you want to serve. If you are blindly sending out resumes to every company with a letterhead, then you are acting like Door number 1's sales pro. You may be thinking, "I've got to get a job. I have GOT TO GET A JOB NOW!" And, to you, any job will do. Any job that issues paychecks every two weeks is just fine for you.

BUT, that's not going to work today in this economy.

Sales Pro Secret #2

Do your homework *before* you apply for a job and definitely before you go to the interview!

Jobs are not a dime a dozen anymore. Employers are looking for the *best* people to hire and they have a large crop to choose from. They want people who are alert, vibrant and alive – they want people who are *excited* about working, not just excited about picking up a paycheck every two weeks. Employers want employees who are excited about contributing to their company, not just those who are excited about what they can get from the company.

In other words, you need to do some work, too. Door number 2 wants to know what your vision is of the future. Who is this gift for? What will this gift mean to your darling?

In a job interview, the same applies. What is the company's vision? Where are you going in the future? How would your position contribute to the company's growth? Why is this position important right now? You can find most of this information on the company's website. Look around, read press releases. Take a look at what the company is doing in the industry. Are they a leader? Are they looking to catch up? How can you contribute in a meaningful way?

When you arrive at the interview, then you can ask more specific questions about your position and how it relates to the company. Before you go, you want to think about how you can *serve that company?* What value do *you* bring to their vision? What skills do you possess that enable you to help the company achieve their goals? Does this company align with what is most important to you? If so, common ground will be easier to achieve.

Day 1 Recap

1.   Get behind Door number 2 and adopt a *sincere, service, sales* mindset. Think of your favorite sales person and begin to see selling as a *good thing* that *helps employers* figure out which person they want to hire – YOU!

2.   Be mindful of when you are thinking of yourself instead of others. Do this all day long and notice when you are thinking about yourself instead of focusing on others.

3.   Make a list of three (ONLY THREE) companies you really want to work with. It doesn't matter if they have a job posted. Identify THREE companies to begin your job search. And if you have been in Fortune 500 for 50 years, remember, there are mid-sized companies that are equally as successful that could be just right for you. *Read Greg's story in Day 9 about *changing your mind about what you think you really want,* for more on this.

Day 1

WORKSHEET

Use a separate piece of paper to answer the following questions or use your notes function. Download these worksheets online in print-ready format in the <u>VIRTUAL APPENDIX</u>.

1. What do you envision for your life? The next five years? The next ten?

2. Think back to a time when you were passionate. What gets you excited? What about the work you do gets your juices pumping?

3. Write down your top three company picks. Does their passion match your passion?

P.S. Those who get the job do the work. If you have not filled this out, do it now!

Day

2

Getting Ready to Move

Yesterday, you reworked your mindset about being a sales professional and how you can serve a future employer by selling yourself.

Today, you are going to get ready to move and ready yourself for something to happen.

Sales Pro Secret #3

Sales professionals keep moving even when things don't seem to be happening

Successful sales people (of which you will be one when you follow these simple steps) know that selling is not all about getting someone to buy. Much of selling is being available when things are ready to happen. To do this, you must show up every day for that something that can happen.

Beginning with today – Day 2 – from now on until you get a job, you will get up like you would every day for a regular job. If that is 5:30 am or 6:00 am, then so be it. You will get up and do exactly what you would do if you had a real job to go to. For right now, your REAL JOB is getting a job, so consider yourself hired!

You are the boss in this job of getting a job, so you must be accountable to yourself. If you aren't great at being accountable to yourself, enlist some friends to support you in this. Make a date for coffee at Starbucks or Denny's and, trust me on this, there's a reason to this crucial step.

Rise at the time you normally would, and address the three S's… Shower, Shave and Shine. Dress in work clothes, comb your hair, and coif your hair just like you would if you were going to work. If you wear bunny slippers at work, then go with those, but if you don't, put the pumps on. Have a good breakfast, and do exactly what you would do if you were going to your last job.

Now, it is time to go to your current job of getting a job. Let's do a quick inventory to ensure you have all of your supplies for your job:

Resume (written in a sales way that highlights your value – see VIRTUAL APPENDIX)

Cover Letter (written in a way that conveys you understand how you can contribute to the company – see VIRTUAL APPENDIX)

List of THREE companies you want to work with

Phone

Computer (available at the library if you do not have one)

Take your list of three companies and now think about all of the people you know. Write these people's names down. See the VIRTUAL APPENDIX for a breakdown of areas of where you might have met these people. Write down every person you can think of. Do not judge any of them. I don't care if you accidentally backed over your neighbor's cat and you think she doesn't like you, put her name down. There's a reason for this.

Sales Pro Secret #4

Sales professionals take care of the details…even when they don't want to

If you are tempted to skip this – don't. This is a very important part of the process. This is going to get your mind geared up for what you need to find your job. Is getting a job important to you? You bet it is! So, get out the pad of paper or the computer and make out your list of people.

DO NOT PASS UNTIL YOU HAVE COMPLETED THIS STEP.

And, if I haven't made myself clear, *how you handle these little steps says a lot about how you are going to handle the bigger process of finding a job.* If you will do these steps – IN ORDER – and trust me, then this job of getting a job will be a short-lived experience!

If you've created your list in earnest, then you should be looking at a list of approximately 250 to 500 names. On average, most people know about 500 people with the Bell curve average hovering around 250 people.

DO NOT WORRY; I am not going to ask you to call all of these people! This is simply for you to have the people you know at the top of your mind. Thus, the reason why they must be dug up from the recesses of your mind.

Next, take a look at your list of THREE COMPANIES and who do you know on your list that works at or with someone at that company? Just let it come to you. Make a mark by the people on the list. If you do not know anyone, then don't worry about it. I have something else for you.

Sales Pro Secret #5

Sales professionals help others get what they want

We interrupt this book for a service announcement for your mind. If you are feeling queasy about the idea of calling someone to ask for a job. Stop right now. You are not calling ANYONE to ask for a job. You would only be calling to ask someone if they know about a company. You would be calling to get *information*. And, in that call, you will also be willing to help and to reciprocate their generosity.

Sales pros know that most people are happy to help others. In fact, most people are energized by helping others. So, forget Door number 1 because that is the only sales professional no one wants to help.

Sales Pro Secret #6

Sales professionals warm up and save their best leads for last

Now it is time to make some phone calls. If you are like many people who have been unemployed for a while, then you may have been hiding out in your house. Today may be the first day you took a shower and dressed up. Perhaps you have not been around people or talked to anyone on the phone. If so, make a warm-up call to get in the groove. Call someone you know, like and trust and who knows, likes and trusts you and warm-up.

Remember, sales professionals do not focus on themselves during the call. Call them, ask how they are doing, tell them you were thinking about them, and ask if there's anything you can do to help them. Then, they will *naturally* ask if there's anything they can do to help you. At this point, let them know that you are focused on getting at job at YOUR THREE COMPANIES and ask if they know anyone who might know someone there or anyone who might know about getting a job there.

The reason for the three companies is three-fold. 1. It helps the people you are talking to focus in on THREE targets so they can *help* you in a *specific* way. 2. It helps *you* focus on the three companies you really want as well. 3. It helps others tell others quickly, easily and refer you.

After your warm-up, you will feel better. It will feel easier. You might even feel some momentum that naturally comes with getting dressed for work and getting right to your 'job' first thing in the morning.

Continue for a minimum of one hour. Take a break. Continue for another hour. Make a note of any 'ideas' or 'people' that pop into your mind at any given time. Keep a pad of paper handy and jot those people down. CALL THEM. And, CALL them TODAY, not tomorrow. Do EVERYTHING you can TODAY because you are *at work*, remember?

If you do not know anyone on your list *well*, then call people you know who are looking for jobs. Call the people you know that are most LIKE YOU. Talk to them and ask them about what they are doing, what they are looking for. OFFER to be of service to *them*. Make coffee dates with those that feel appropriate to meet with. DO NOT meet with everyone and fall into the trap of busy-ness. Stay focused.

Day 2 Recap

1. Rise at your regular workday time.
2. Shower, Shave & Starbucks.
3. Add to your list of supplies, if you do not currently have them.
4. Create your list of 250.
5. Call those who may know someone at the company where you want to get a job.
6. Contact people you know, *who are like you,* who may also be looking for a job and let them know which companies you want to work for. Offer to help others.
7. Set appointments to meet with others.

Day 2

WORKSHEET

Remember the game six degrees of separation? Well, the Rule of 250 powers that game so that you can skip, hop and leap across vast numbers of people to arrive at your destination faster! Use this sheet to help your mind focus and create your list of the 250 people YOU know. *See VIRTUAL APPENDIX for form.*

Day

3

Building Your Sell "You" Toolkit

Welcome to Day 3. I'm sure you have showered, shaved and Starbucks-ed yourself for the day. Yesterday, you created your list of 250 people – at least one of which will know someone at one of the three companies where *you* want to work.

Today, you will be building out your sales toolkit. For most job seekers, the number one tool in their toolkit would be their *resume*, and while this is a very important tool, it is not the most *essential*. Today and every day – even after you get your job – the most important tool in your toolkit is *you*.

A new sales relationship is like any brand-new relationship. The employer knows nothing about you, and vice versa. Selling is about creating a relationship where none existed before. You build a relationship by creating trust with others. The way for others to trust you is to first trust yourself, and from that place you will show up and be confident. It is imperative for you to believe in yourself – no matter how long it has been since you left your last job – and to believe you can and *will* get a new job. Today is the day to put to rest all of the things that have happened in your job search; time to eliminate all of the ideas you've started to believe as a result of what has seemingly not been working.

Sales Pro Secret #7

Sales professionals give their attitude as much attention as they do their support resources

Successful sales people don't perform the 'shoulds' or 'have to's' consistently or with much exuberance, but they do 'want to's' all the time with no reminders. To adopt a winning attitude, shift your 'have to's' to 'want to's' as you look for a job.

To turn a 'should' into a 'want to,' remember that every step is taking you toward what you most want – a job! And, not just any old job, but a job at a company of *your choice!* Now, *that's* something to be *excited* about. You know you want to get the interview or the job, and the way to get each of those is to take the steps I'm giving you here and to bring a *winning attitude.*

Besides your winning attitude, you will need to bring your sharp as a tack winning mindset. This includes a list of all of the things you do extraordinarily well, the benefits you can bring to the employer and the self-esteem to share these without feeling self-conscious. If you are like most of us, you have spent your life focusing on everything you do not do well and rarely spend time celebrating what is best about you.

If you don't know what you do well, think about your last review and the positive comments that you received. Think about what others are always saying about you, such as, *Tom is always prepared and ready to go. Mary is great at getting people to work as a team. Mike has the greatest ideas and know how to make them happen.* When you use *other people's words,* then you paint a picture of what is best about you that also will *feel* authentic to you because you have heard them *spoken* to you by someone else.

Sales Pro Secret #8

Sales professionals focus on their strengths and celebrate their unique abilities and let go of worrying about their so-called weaknesses

Even the best sales professionals often spend much of their time thinking about their weaknesses and how they can improve. The result is they often spend an inordinate amount of time focused on what they do poorly instead of what they do well, which just works to leave them feeling inadequate and ill-equipped to develop strong relationships with people who might be interested in working with them.

As we grow up, we are taught to learn from our mistakes. While I agree with this to a point, I believe you can shift your thinking to learn from your successes as well. Think of your top five interview successes. What did you do well? What worked? Where did you shine? In addition to what worked in an interview situation, think of your top five successes on the job. Where were you a superstar? Stay focused on these and soon, you will feel more courageous and stronger mentally for the task at hand. Take a moment and jot down these moments:

1. ____
2. ____
3. ____
4. ____
5. ____

Successful sales people reflect the Six Cs of Selling:

Committed: Do you love what you do? Do you wake up, ready to meet the next prospect, and ready to serve him or her to your best ability? Anyone can be a sales schmo, but not everyone is committed enough to be a sales dynamo.

Consistent: You already know the fortune is in the follow-up. And, how you do anything is how you do everything. If you can't be consistent in sales, then likely you can't be consistent in customer service follow-up, customer calls and everything else involved in being a top producer. Commit to be consistent!

Curious: Do you have a genuine curiosity for learning about other people? This one trait can turn sales calls into sales conversions. Be curious and ask about others. Listen intently and you'll learn all you need to know to be a fantastic salesperson.

Contagious: I'm not talking about being Bozo the Clown here, but I am talking about being enthusiastic, energized and being who you are. Buyers love people who are passionate; their excitement is contagious.

Concise: You don't have all day, neither does your customer. Get to the point about your info and be direct. This helps your buyer to *remember* important information so he or she can take it back to other decision makers in the company. Keep the conversation concise and focused on what is important for the customer.

Caring: Here's the real ABC of selling…**A**lways **B**e **C**aring. People don't care how much you know until they know how much you care. Show you care by listening, by remembering important details and by consistently following up!

Where do you rate yourself from 1 to 10 (10 being highest) for each of these? Today is all about strengthening your Sell 'You' Toolkit. There is an employer out there who is looking just for 'you.' This toolkit will ensure the employers see 'you' so they can hire you!

Day 3 Recap

1. Rise at your regular workday time.
2. Shower, Shave & Starbucks.
3. Add to your list of supplies if you do not currently have them.
4. Review your sales attitude.
5. Inventory your selling strengths, best job interviews and your job successes.
6. Rate yourself by the Six C's of Selling.
7. Continue to contact people you know, *who are like you.* Let them know which companies you want to work for. Offer to connect them to others.

Day 3

WORKSHEET

Download this worksheet online in print-ready format in the VIRTUAL APPENDIX.

Day

4

Preparing to Market Yourself, and Land a Job NOW

Imagine a day in the life of your prospective employer. Resumes flowing out of inboxes and mailboxes every day. Cover letters look the same, sound the same. Everywhere the employer looks there are resumes, cover letters that blend homogenously into a big ball of blandness.

Why?

For the most part, this is because most people want to *blend in* and *fit in* with others. And, while that might be a great strategy once you *get the job*, it's a disastrous job hunting strategy. When you are looking for a job, you want to *stand out*, so you will have the opportunity to meet the prospective employer to actually interview to get the job.

Put yourself in the employer's shoes. Boring resume after boring resume. A stack of papers with ink splattered across the page with the same words, the same cover letter template, the sameness is blinding. All of a sudden, there's a cover letter with a little extra something special. The letter talks about last quarter's earnings, perhaps a thoughtful idea that indicates the person is actually thinking about the *business* and what would benefit the *business*. Suddenly, the sleepy prospective employer (or maybe the hiring manager or HR person) feels livelier...awake. You've done it! You've stood apart from the others, and for all of the right reasons. Soon, a phone call is being placed to you for an interview. Putting yourself in the employer's shoes is the first step to building the right marketing mindset. Do set yourself apart for all of the right reasons. Don't set yourself apart for all of the wrong ones.

Sales Pro Secret #9

Sales professionals stand out in a crowd and leave a memorable, authentic, lasting impression

Leaving a lasting impression requires learning some job hunting dos and don'ts. Sales pros know that a lasting impression originates from genuine authentic creativity. Do NOT use someone else's. It can be tempting to want to use a gimmick or clever idea that works for someone else. Today's headlines tout crazy ideas that have landed people jobs, yet those people used their own brand of creativity. Don't be tempted to copy someone else's ideas. Only represent yourself in a way that is true for you. By being yourself, you will leave the most memorable impression. And, if you are truly a fit, then the job will be yours.

The name of the getting hired game is to focus on benefits to the employer for hiring you. Many job seekers are like Sales Pro #1 – it's all about *them*. They want to know how much they are going to make, what kind of benefits they are going to get, and what they have to *do* to get these goodies. A sales savvy interview focuses on highlighting and spotlighting what *you* bring to the table and gives your prospective employer a vision of what kind of employee you could be for his/her and what kind of results can be expected from what you bring to the table.

In this job market, where there are many more candidates than there are jobs, you must come to the interview bringing more than the requisite "yes, I can do that," you must reach beyond this threshold and go into the employer's world and offer an idea of what else you can offer. But, as I said before, this is not about being something you are not. This book is about helping you bring your own brand of specialness to the table and this gives you tips and pointers of what to bring and what to leave at the interview door.

Remember Sales Professional Door #2 – the sales pro who is focused on the client. In this case, you are the sales pro and your employer to be is the client. The easiest way to sell is to put yourself in your client's shoes. What would help your *employer* hire you?

Yesterday, you made a list of your best job interviews and your best on-the-job successes, now you want to create sound bites of these so you can quickly and easily access the information without talking too long, stumbling on your words or becoming stymied due to nerves. For each of the following, create your top-of-mind sound bites.

Top Results-Getting, On-the-Job Successes: This is where you take what you do best and *quantify* the results. This is all about speaking the employer's language. For example, let's say that you are a great manager of teams. To quantify this, you would focus on a *measurable* that illustrates this. You might say, "Within six months of working with my team, productivity increased 20 percent." Note: Do *not* make these up. Only quantify true numbers. For each position, identify your top five success stories. Include these on your resume, and then *write down* what you would say in an interview. Keep your answer to a minute or less. You can always add details if asked.

Your Super Talents: Every person does at least two or three things better than anyone else. Do you know yours? Yesterday, you listed your strengths. Today, *write down* each one in a way you would share in an interview. If you want, add an example to illustrate each one. These may be linked to your Top Results. That is okay. The idea here is to write them down so you have them 'top-of-mind.'

What You Don't Do Well: Anyone who has been in an interview knows that many employers will ask what your weakness is. While I don't believe this is the most important thing, we can't change the world and how they interview! Therefore, I want you to write down what you believe is your weakness and *then* I want you to talk about how you've used your *talents* to make up for it. In short, I want you to make your weakness a moot point! A confident sales person tells the truth with confidence and then addresses any concern with a *solution*. *Write down* your weakness and then think of an example of how you've made up for it or used a creative solution.

Link Your Passion to the Job. There's nothing more contagious than a passionate person. Personalize the company and the job to your passion.

Think about the job prior to the interview and consider where the opportunity and your passion for the work you do meet. *Write down* why you would love to work at the company, and what you believe you can bring to the company. Add what you admire about the company and why you want to contribute your talents to the company.

When you 'write down' your ideas above, do not 'write.' Just write down what you would speak. If it works for you, you can even tape record your answers and then type them. Or use a program that types what you speak. This exercise helps you 'practice' your answers ahead of time, and when you get there, this practice will allow you to listen fully and intently knowing you are *prepared*.

Day 4 Recap

1.   Rise at your regular workday time.
2.   Shower, Shave & Starbucks.
3.   Add to your list of supplies if you do not currently have them.
4.   Create your interview sound bites.
5.   Call those who may know someone at the company where you want to get a job.
6.   Contact people you know, *who are like you*, who may also be looking for a job and let them know which companies you want to work for.

Day 4

WORKSHEET

Download this worksheet online in print-ready format in the VIRTUAL APPENDIX.

Top Results-Getting, On-the-Job Successes

Position 1:

Position 2:

Position 3:

Position 4:

Position 5:

Your Super Talents

If you slid by yesterday and did not do your homework, take a moment to get in the 'mood' for identifying your super talents. Think about:

1. *Times at work when you felt most passionate. What excited you?*

2. *Times at work when you felt most fulfilled. What gave you a sense of fulfillment?*

3. *Times at work when you felt you could do anything and were in just the right place.*

4. *Times at work when time seemed to evaporate and you lost yourself in your work.*

Now, imagine an employer asking, *"What do you do particularly well?"* Write down what you would say that spotlights what is great about you, include a story that comes to mind, results that you were able to achieve, a comment your boss said about what you did, something a co-worker said to you. Let your mind go and just write what comes to you. You can edit it later so it is more polished. No one sees this except you!

Super Talent 1 Story(ies):

Super Talent 2 Story(ies):

Super Talent 3 Story(ies):

What You Don't Do Well

Often people think what you don't do well is held against you; however, successful people from all walks of life routinely do one to three things well and a host of other things only semi-well. Employers want people who know what they do well, what they don't do well and how to bridge the gap in between. You can answer the 'weakness' question in a way that makes you look strong. Practice writing your answer here so that when the interview comes, it will flow out in a confident way. Write down your weakness and then think of an example of how you've made up for it or used a creative solution to overcome it.

Link Your Passion to the Job

Write down why you would love to work at the company, and what you believe you bring to the company. Add why your passion/talents would be an asset to the company. Visualize how you could make a difference. Be sure to *write it all down!* (There's an important reason why. Do it!)

Day

5

The Job Hunting Landscape Has Changed, and It Hasn't

Twitter, Facebook, LinkedIn, Monster, Careerbuilder – all of these end with .com. If you've been in a job for more than a decade, you may not have even dealt with this new digital job hunting landscape that is filled with resume databanks and pre-screening. And, though the tools are different, the job hunting basics are still the same. This chapter is not meant to be an exhaustive in-depth resource for *how* to use the tools, but rather a new way to look at the landscape that may be a bit overwhelming.

The bottom line is that you get a job from a *person* or *many persons;* you do not get a job from technology – that's the good news! You get to decide if you will work *with* technology or *against it.* Rest assured, you can work with technology – *if you decide to!*

One of the biggest obstacles you will need to overcome with the new technology in the job hunting space is located between your ears in your mind. The technology can be mind-boggling. Instead of focusing on all that you don't know or being overwhelmed by all of the options, stick to the program in this book and stay with the basics. This book relies on the power of *people*, and can help you bypass the impersonal nature of resume databanks. In the resources section, you will find additional resources for specific technology should you need it. And, in this chapter, you will fine-tune the tools of the job-seeking trade.

Now, what hasn't changed are the traditional job-seeking staples:

Resume: You must have a resume. Your resume must spotlight how great you are. Avoid offering a laundry list of 'tasks' or 'responsibilities' you've had in previous positions. Focus on *career milestones, results* and *paint a picture* of what kind of employee you are by using your previous experience as a canvas. *See VIRTUAL APPENDIX for examples.*

Cover Letter: If you are submitting your resume or giving your resume to a friend to hand-deliver to HR, you also will need a cover letter. Many people think of a cover letter as an afterthought; however, I believe a great cover letter is the first place to make a striking impression. The cover letter offers an opportunity for you to use your creativity to stand out. Dare to say something noteworthy. Remember to keep it genuine. *See <u>VIRTUAL APPENDIX</u> for examples.*

30-second Infomercial: As you meet with colleagues and talk to people you know, you want to be ready and prepared with a quick way to share what you are doing now, what you are looking for, which companies you would love to work with and how you can be reached.

Sales Pro Secret #10

Sales professionals know what they do best *first* and then adapt the world to themselves

Remember that your job hunt does not mean you must master every job-seeking resume bank on the internet. This book is about utilizing the person-to-person underground networks that deliver *real jobs* to *real people*. With the tools above, you have everything you need to find a job.

Do not waste your precious energy and time worrying about what you don't know about how technology works and all the tools 'available' today. If and when you come across a tool you must add to your arsenal, you can learn it then, but only then. Do *not* invest in tomorrow's worries today.

One last thing to remember, which may be the hardest to accept is the lack of feedback that the new job hunting landscape offers today. You may have submitted 500 resumes to online job postings and received less than 10 responses to your resume submission. Gone are the days when companies replied with a form letter or email. New job hunters may find this lack of response demoralizing. Don't fall into this trap. Instead of focusing on what may *not* be happening, and I do say *may* because who knows how long each company may interview. One recent job hunter told me that he received a phone call after 8 weeks! Your job until you get a new job is to show up each day full of enthusiasm for your *current job*, which is *getting a job interview.*

Do not stop moving day to day *until* you receive an offer. The most successful job seekers *show up* each day *expecting* something to happen. You can be successful to GET A JOB NOW!

Day 5 Recap

1. Rise at your regular workday time.

2. Shower, Shave & Starbucks.

3. Let go of any technology worries you may have.

4. Review your resume, cover letter and 30-second infomercial to ensure these spotlight you well.

5. Call those who may know someone at the company where you want to get a job.

6. Contact people you know, *who are like you*, who may also be looking for a job and let them know which companies you want to work for.

Day 5

WORKSHEET

Download this worksheet online in print-ready format in the <u>VIRTUAL APPENDIX</u>.

4-Step Formula for a Winning 30-second Job Seeking Infomercial

In networking situations, people announce their names, their company names and also what type of business they are in or what they can do to serve others. This infomercial is *exactly* the same and with your homework from the last three days, you will be able to complete *your* infomercial in record time!

Step 1 – What is your name?

Step 2 – What is a snappy way (one sentence or less) to highlight the overall talents you bring to the table? So, let's say that you are a computer programmer who is very creative and also able to figure out any problem in programming. You might say, *I'm a programming wizard who can solve the most difficult programming challenges, no matter what, I never give up.* Write yours down here:

Step 3 – Who do you want to work for? Remember you three companies? Now's the time to put those in! It might sound like, "I am looking for a person who can connect me to a person at Company A, Company B or Company C." Write yours in a way that feels natural here:

Step 4 – The memory minder. Keep your close memorable. Say something that will help people remember you. If you can link up a visual cue to what you say, it will work even better. Something like, "If you know of a person in these companies, think of me as the Inspector Gadget for programming. I've got a tool or a solution for just about anything. You can reach me at ___________ insert the way for them to get in touch with you.

Day

6

The Interview

You've just gotten the call and it's time for your interview. What do you do? One of the things that drives me crazy is when I hear stories from well-intentioned people who have spent hours upon hours to get their foot in the door of the company they desire to work with and then blow it because they have not *prepared* for the interview. These good people literally threw their opportunity right down the drain.

Do not let this be you.

Sales Pro Secret #11

Sales professionals prepare to maximize opportunity

Successful sales people plan to be prepared and to maximize the opportunity to be successful. Prepare for the interview with the same enthusiasm you have for going to work each day. This is one of the biggest steps standing between what you and what you want.

Here are tips to prepare for the interview:

Read about the company. Visit the website and read press releases, the history and any other news you can find about what the company is doing. *Use the Interview Questions form from this chapter for more tips.*

Be curious. What do you want to know about the company? Look for it on the Internet, and write down any questions you still have that you could not find in your research. *Use the Cultivate Curiosity form from this chapter for more tips.*

Investigate the competition. What companies compete with your prospective employer? What are these companies doing? What captures your curiosity about how these activities may affect your prospective employer?

Where does the company fit? Where does the company fit in its industry? Where does it fit in the marketplace? Where does the company fit in the community? In the world?

Where do you fit? Where do you fit in with the company and its activities? How can you be the answer for your prospective employer's current challenges? Where can you lend your talents for the company's success?

Review your sound bites. If you have followed this book's process, you will have your sound bites ready and can review those now and adjust to match the company's unique opportunity.

Prepare a fresh resume for your in-person interview. Arrive prepared with an additional copy or two of your resume. Applicants often believe the employer will have a copy, and sometimes employers are humans, too, and misplace resumes. You can help a prospect avoid embarrassment by having a fresh copy handy.

Arrive on time. You have one chance to make a lasting impression. Arrive on time or early, but do not arrive too early. Plan to arrive no more than 10 minutes early, unless asked to arrive otherwise.

Dress the part. You can overdress and be excused, but if you underdress you've just blown your chance to make a lasting impression. Gentlemen, please wear a suit and tie. Ladies, wear a matching skirt and jacket or suit or dress. If you do not have the funds to dress appropriately, do whatever you can to borrow clothes to make a lasting impression. Do not let anything stand in your way of getting a job now!

Power-up Your Passion. Bring your winning attitude to the interview. Remember, you are just as valuable as the employer is. You have talents the prospective employer can utilize to become even more successful. Even if you *feel desperate* to find a job, power up your passion and belief in what you can offer the employer.

Sales Pro Secret #12

Sales professionals begin with the end in mind

Successful sales people prepare, plan and project into the future what they expect to accomplish. Prior to going to the interview, imagine yourself answering every question easily, feeling comfortable in the interview. See yourself talking to the employer and offering good ideas. Picture yourself doing your very best – arriving on time, looking the part and leaving a lasting impression. Picture the prospective employer calling you with a job offer.

Day 6 Recap

1.   The night before, visualize a great interview. Address any gaps that you notice.

2.   Get a good night's rest the night before.

3.   Rise at your regular workday time.

4.   Shower, Shave & Starbucks.

5.   Let go of any interview worries you may have.

6.   Prepare for the interview using this chapter as a guide.

7.   Have all of your interview tools ready the night before – resume, clothes, gas in the car.

Day 6

WORKSHEET

Download this worksheet online in print-ready format in the <u>VIRTUAL APPENDIX</u>.

Getting Ready for the Interview Questions

Use this form to guide you in researching the company online. Complete what you can from your online research and then compile any unanswered questions for the interview.

1.   Key management in the organization: (CEO, President, Other relevant decision makers – where does your 'prospective boss' fall in the organization?)

a.   CEO –

b.   President –

c.   Decision Maker –

d.   Decision Maker –

e.   Who you are interviewing with –

2.   Is the company privately or publicly held? Is it financially sound?

3.   How long has the company been in business? Have there been recent mergers or acquisitions? If so, with which company?

4.   Who is the company's primary competitor? Look for the type of company and research who else comes up in a search for that type of company. Who else would be competing with the company? How does this affect the position you are applying for? Your prospective boss's job?

5.   What other companies has this company done work with in the past?

6.   What do you know about this company that makes you believe you would be a good fit for the company? Be sure to *write it down*. This will solidify your answer in your mind.

7.   What is your strategy to get this job? Will you focus on what you can do for the company? Will you point out opportunities you see? How will you handle this interview to ensure the interviewer sees you as the best choice?

8.   How is this position tied to your personal vision (you created this just a few days ago)? Write down what you would say if the interviewer asks, "Where do you see yourself in 5 years?" And, tie it to the company.

9.   What other information is pertinent to this interview?

Be Curious Questions

Top talent is always in demand, so an interview is a two-way street where you are also interviewing the prospective employer to see if the company is a good fit for *you*.

1. What is the best part of the business at this point in time? What opportunities are you excited about?

2. What is the most difficult part of your business at this point in time? How would that affect the department or group I would be in?

3. Who do you consider major competitors in your industry?

4. Have you always been in this type of business?

5. How is the company viewed within the industry?

6. What would you like to be different about the department? About the company?

7. How do you see my skills assisting in your current goals?

8. What is the most exciting project the department (or company) has done recently?

9. How do you keep up-to-date in the industry?

10. How does technology play a part in your business?

11. Identify your three top values and ask questions to solicit information to see if you are a fit for the company, for example, if work-life balance is important to you, you might ask: *What is the company's view of work-life balance?* If personal growth and development is important to you, you might ask: *Does the company invest in annual continuing education for each employee?* You can link a question like this to one of your strengths as well, for example: *Because I easily pick up new technology, I enjoy staying at the leading edge of what is new in the industry. Does the company invest in annual continuing education for each employee?*

How To Be a Good Listener

1.   Listening begins with *wanting to hear what the other person is saying.* Be present and LISTEN until you are asked to speak. Do not try to rehearse your answers while the person is speaking, this will lead you to looking distracted. If you have *written down* everything I've suggested, then your answers will be *in your head.* Trust your preparation!

2.   Strive to be an empathetic listener. This requires you to let go of your wants and needs and to simply *be* in the conversation. Strive to make a *connection* and let go of trying to *get the job.* If you make a connection, you will likely get the job if you are qualified. Your focus is on *connecting,* not on trying to prove yourself. An empathetic listener answers questions and asks relevant questions as well. There is a give and a take to the conversation that imparts, *I care about you regardless of whether or not I get the job.* Curiosity is naturally empathetic.

3.   When you want people to listen to you:

a.   Say something worthy of hearing.

b.   Speak *their* language in terms *they understand*

c.   Take them out of where they are and invite them into a conversation with you

d.   Establish that what you are going to say is important to *them* – focus on what *they* are focused on (again, this means you are going to have to let go of trying to 'get' the job – do your best to connect)

4.   Use positive vocabulary instead of negative vocabulary. This is particularly important if you have been laid off and the prospect asks what happened with your last job. You need to have your story ready so that you sound like you are okay with what happened and are eager to move to a new place to contribute your talents. Avoid negative judgments of any past employers, past projects, etc.

5.   Use pictures to paint a story, if possible and if this feels authentic to you. Use verbs with action instead of 'be' verbs. Instead of saying I was, I did, I am, say I managed, I led, I created. Use dynamic language to speak and you will stand a cut above all other candidates. Using action language

is more energized than 'be' verbs. By adding pictures to your answers, you will draw the interviewer into another state of mind. For example, you might say, I led a team of two men and three women for 18 months. During that time, we created 20 products – 5 more than then the president challenged us to do. By using specifics, the mind is focused in on the numbers and you become more *memorable.*

These few techniques can leave your interviewer feeling powerfully charged. There's a saying that goes like this: People won't remember what you say, but they will always remember how you made them feel. Use these techniques to leave a lasting impression.

Are You a Good Listener? Quiz

1.   I make eye contact when I am being interviewed.   T/F

2.   I lean forward, nod and smile when listening .   T/F

3.   I take notes that I can refer to later.   T/F

4.   I am conscious of the interviewer's body language.   T/F

5.   I am relaxed and at ease at interviews.   T/F

6.   I allow the person speaking to finish their sentences and do not interrupt. T/F

7.   I never cut a person off to give a quick answer.   T/F

8.   I feel comfortable and breathe normally during an interviewer.   T/F

9.   I am not thinking of my answers ahead of time.   T/F

10. I notice the back and forth rhythm to the conversation.   T/F

Grade Yourself

9-10 True Answers: *You are a GREAT LISTENER. Congratulations!*

6-9 True Answers: *You listen most of the time, but there's room for improvement.*

Less than 5 True Answers: Stop talking. Start listening!

If you scored less than a 9 or 10 on this quiz, consider *role playing* with a friend or loved one to practice calming down, focusing and letting go of preconceived ideas of trying to control the flow of information.

Increasing Environmental Awareness

You are interviewing the interviewer and also gathering information so you can decide if this company is a good fit for you. Here are a few suggestions to increase your awareness of the company's culture and environment.

As you walk through, notice:

1. What do you see when you walk into the company?
2. What do you hear?
3. What is the emotional climate?
4. Are these happy people? Are they open? Closed? Are they more similar to you? More dissimilar? Would you feel comfortable coming here every day for work?
5. Do employees seem active, productive and engaged?
6. Is the office neat and well-kept?
7. What is the overall 'feeling' you get in the office? Do you like this?

Often, interviewees are so preoccupied with their own self-conscious behavior they miss information about the company when they go to interview. Use these questions to focus you on 'listening' to the environment so you can know if this is a fit for you or not.

Day

7

The Fortune is in the Follow-up

In today's technology-driven world, high-touch is often woefully out of style. While everyone else is sending an email thank-you, *you* can stand out by sending a thank-you through the good ol' postal service. Sales pros have a saying that is true: The fortune is in the follow-up.

Your job interview does not end at the conclusion of your interview. Your interview includes the follow-up. In fact, the job is often secured in the follow-up. Be sure to follow-up!

Sales Pro Secret #13

Sales professionals Put as much energy and attention into the follow-up as they do in getting the initial contact

There's a popular saying that goes like this: *How you do anything is how you do everything.* Your follow-up and what you choose to do or not to do say as much about you as the way you interview. Plan to follow-up in a way that reflects your own personal style.

At the end of the interview, ask the interviewer when s/he expects to make a hiring decision. Say this in a thoughtful way as if you need to know so you can follow-up, not in a desperate way. Regardless of what the answer is, thank the interviewer for his or her time. Many companies are interviewing for as long as three months at a time, so do not act deflated if you get an answer such as, "We won't be hiring for another month. You are the first applicant we are hiring!" Be positive, proactive and thank the person. Ask *permission* to follow-up so you will not feel strange when you do. You might say, "That sounds great. Would it be okay with you if I contact you around that time if I have not heard from you?" At that point, the interviewer will either give you permission, point you to the person you need to call instead or give you his/her permission. Be sure to ask for a business card so you will have the person's correct name spelling and contact information.

When you complete the interview, your first thought should be to determine how you will follow-up to thank the person interviewed for the position. As I mentioned, high-touch in this world can help you stand above other applicants. Consider sending a through the mail correspondence thank you note. In the note do the following:

Thank the person by name – *last name.* Mr. or Mrs. Interviewer, *unless* s/he asked you to call him or her by his or her first name.

Express your sincerest thoughts from the interview. For example: *I appreciate your time and I believe my skills would be a match to your upcoming project.*

Let the person know you listened to what s/he said and impart your enthusiasm. I look forward to possibly being part of your team, which sounds like a group of people committed to excellence in the _________ industry.

Do NOT be too personal or overly presumptuous in the thank you note. Leave out personal details, such as, "You are the only company that has called me so I can be available any time you need me." Or over presumptuous, such as, "I'm sure you will see that I am exactly the person you have been searching for. I am the best there is in my field." There's a line between confident and overly presumptuous. Don't cross it unless this is truly your personality and style. It can backfire on you.

Be sure to write a thank you for EACH person who interviewed you. This may seem like a lot of effort, but don't forget, these people will likely talk to EACH OTHER when they discuss their hiring decision. Therefore, do each of these steps for EACH person. DO NOT use a boiler plate thank you note. If you do, they may see that you wrote the same things to each person. Remember, in selling, you are looking for a connection with EACH *person*. Make your best impression with each person along the way and the bigger picture of getting the job takes care of itself.

Even if the job doesn't appear to be a fit, write a thank you note, anyway. With six degrees of separation, you just never know how people are connected and if a person may refer you to someone else at another company. If you think this is a stretch, I have heard stories just like this!

Mail the thank you the evening of the interview if at all possible. If not, then NO LATER than the NEXT day. You want to look like a person who is organized, conscientious and has their act together. This can make a huge impression on the interviewer(s). In fact, this may be the tenth degree that pushes you over the edge if it is really close between applicants. Remember, you are the boss of your job hunting!

Make a genuine connection. Amidst the sheer volume of people who are looking for a job these days, there are many websites touting templates that you can use to thank your prospective employer. The key to making lasting impression is the *connection;* it is not about doing the thank you. This is similar to how people address cover letters – wham bam, that's done kind of mentality. I've included a formula for a winning, empathetic thank you note that is derived from your *experience* with the person in today's worksheet. Use that, and skip boilerplate templates that all sound the same.

Be SURE to proofread your thank you note and ensure it does not have any errors – grammar or spelling. If you aren't sure, type up your note on your computer and then write it on a hand-written thank you note. This way, you can use the computer to check spelling and grammar. Still, you will need to READ your thank you aloud to ensure you do not have any errors.

Regardless of how sure you may be that the job is yours, don't stop your job hunting efforts. Continue to meet with people who are like you and like you. Be sure to mark your calendar to follow-up with the prospective employer when s/he indicated a hiring decision would be made. If you follow-up and are told a hiring decision has not been made, again, ask for permission to follow-up and ask what the best way to follow-up is. Be sure to mark your calendar again.

Human nature is what it is. Selling a product or service is really no different than selling yourself. According to a McGraw Hill Lap Study, 46% of sales people call once and quit. Another 25% call and quit. A third group of 12% make three calls and quit. Just over 10% keep calling until they get the sale. When you consider 80% of all sales are made after *five* calls, it becomes *clear* that the determined, politely persistent, patient person is going to win. And, it is no wonder why 90% of *all* sales are made by only 10% of the sales people. They are the ones that are in the right place at the right time for the deal!

The same thing applies to getting a job. That's why I've made it very clear you need to get up every day and embrace the day like it is a *work day* – it is! – your work is getting a job. Remember, the fortune *is* in the follow-up as this study shows. Be sure you FOLLOW UP!

Day 7 Recap

1.   Rise at your regular workday time.
2.   Shower, Shave & Starbucks.
3.   Follow-up with your prospective employer (if you haven't already!)
4.   Address any phone calls, additional interviews. Do not stop until you have a firm offer in hand.
5.   Expect a job offer, but do not get tied into only one opportunity. This can save you from going into a downward spiral of disappointment. Stay optimistic.
6.   Call those who may know someone at the company where you want to get a job.
7.   Contact people you know, *who are like you*, who may also be looking for a job and let them know which companies you want to work for.

Day 7

WORKSHEET

Download this worksheet online in print-ready format in the VIRTUAL APPENDIX.

Formula for a Winning Thank You Note

Step 1 – Thank the person by their last name (unless s/he indicated otherwise in the interview). For example: *Dear Mr. Johnson.*

Step 2 – Include a relevant piece of information about the job and/or upcoming project and tie your talents to it. For example: *I am excited about your upcoming XYZ project, which sounds like it will require a team with diverse talents. I believe my skill of _________ could be an asset to the team.*

Step 3 – Include something you respect about the company or the interviewer. For example: *I respect the work that XYZ company believes in making a difference in the world and would like to work for a company that reflects my own values.*

Step 4 – Close the thank you with optimism. For example: *I look forward to hearing from you. Thank you again for you time.*

Thank You Note Checklist

1. Followed the Thank You Note formula.
2. Sent a separate Thank You Note to each interviewer.
3. Mailed the Thank You Notes the *evening of* or NO LATER than the next day.
4. Marked a follow-up date on your calendar.

Day

8

Overcoming Obstacles

By far, the toughest part of the job search is overcoming obstacles that crop up. One of the most difficult aspects of looking for a job in this day and age is the 'limbo' that many job seekers feel. Companies are bombarded with resumes and applicants, and with electronic resume submissions, you may find that you send your resume into a 'black hole' only to never get a response – negative or otherwise – or you might go to interviews and never hear back. As a result, job seekers tend to never 'know' where they stand. This is drastic difference from job hunting just 20 years ago.

This book is designed to empower you and put you into a proactive stance of *connecting with others to find a job* (vs. doing the resume scattershoot), *give you the tools to reconnect with prospective employers after the interview* (instead of waiting for these overworked companies to remember to contact you), and *design your job hunt based on what you want* (vs. what is out there that you can choose from).

Sales Pro Secret #14

Sales professionals create their opportunities by reinventing the game

Successful sales people realize there is the game that every Joe Blow is playing, and then there's the game the superstars are playing. This entire book is about reinventing the job search game by putting the power and action steps in *your* hands. One of the most demoralizing feelings job seekers who are playing the regular job search game is that they have no control and no power to 'get a job.' This is just one perspective – the perspective of people who are job seeking in a 'reactive' way. By following these guidelines, you will reinvent the game by being proactive and *taking action*, staying in *motion* and creating opportunity through your *preparedness*.

In this chapter, I will address the most common obstacles I see with job seekers today.

Obstacle #1 – Job Seeker Depression

Still, there may be days when you find yourself getting down. So this is
what the top sales people do, *they do what they need to do anyway.* Whether
you put on a favorite song and dance while you brush your teeth or you call a
friend to cheer you up, you *must keep moving.* If you are seriously depressed,
get professional help. If you have the job seeker blues, get into action.
Studies show that people who stay in action not only feel better, but feel more
optimistic in general. If you keep moving, tomorrow will not be the same as
today, and because it is not the same, more opportunities are bound to come
your way.

Obstacle #2 – Lapse in Time Between Previous Employer and Now

Remember, this time of job seeking is different than all others.
Employers understand gaps in employment history. Do not take on the idea
that you will be judged for not being able to secure a job right away. For jobs
over $100,000 per year, the average time to locate a new position is nearly 18
months! Also, you bring a complete package that offers the employer
immense value. The 'totality' of you includes: People you know, Talents you
possess, Knowledge you've acquired, and much, much more. You are
valuable beyond your lapse in employment. Remember this! One question
employers may ask you is … *What have you been doing with your time?*
Always be honest and share what is *true,* and also highlight any projects
you've taken on in the meantime. For example, one job seeker I know
volunteered to help a friend from church convert his company database into a
new type of system the job seeker was training himself to learn. The project
allowed him to put his newly-developed skills to work, and also to help a
friend whose business had also declined during the recession. This simple
answer led to his new employer offering him a job – demanding those same
skills he had just acquired. What you do with your unemployment is
reflective of who you are as a person. Are you making the most of your time?

Obstacle #3 – Poor Attitude

You may be mad, frustrated, angry, feeling the effects of poor me, but whatever emotion that is eating your lunch, the overall malaise can be labeled 'poor attitude.' The first step to overturn a poor attitude is to figure out what's eating you. Narrow down how you feel by naming it. Then accept that is how you are feeling. Decide what you would like to feel next.

One of the most important things you can do during this job seeking time is to cut yourself a break. Take time to take care of yourself. Yes, get up and do all of the things I'm encouraging you to do, but also use this time to do what you haven't had time to do. Go to the park. Take a walk. Have a coffee with a friend you miss. Reconnect with a favorite hobby. All work and no play make Jack or Jill boring. One of the mistakes job seekers make is staying in seeking mode 24/7. This is not going to get you the job faster; it's just going to give you a poor attitude. Mind your mind and give yourself breaks.

Another strategy may involve meeting with a mastermind group to keep each person in the group focused and uplifted. Many such groups have sprung up for every level of employee, including executives who are networking to tap into the golden underground of business job referrals.

Obstacle #4 – Many Job Interviews, No Job Offers

This is a difficult proposition for most, but it doesn't have to be the end of the road. The first thing you need to do is contact the interviewer and ask for a short call so you can ask what you could have done better. Yes, these people are busy, but it is doubtful other job seekers are asking for this time. Be politely persistent and ask for just 10 to 15 minutes of the interviewer's time. Don't be desperate, yet *do* be direct and say why you are calling. When you get your 10 minutes, focus on *the interview* – do not put the person on the defensive, i.e., *Why didn't you hire me?* Rather, focus on what could have made a difference *during the interview*. You might ask if there were skills that would have made a difference, too. Keep the conversation *neutral* and think of it like a fact-finding mission. Just the facts. This effort can do two things: 1. Set you up in case something falls through for the person hired, and 2. Help you improve your interview skills.

Obstacle #5 – Wondering If It is Time to Take Another Route?

People who are wondering if it is time to do something else other than get another job mostly likely have that alternative tucked in the back of their mind. If you have done the steps in this book, there's no doubt that you have gotten at least one interview. However, if you got there and something nagged at you to consider another option, take a look at it. Many people during this recession used it as an opportunity to start consulting or to work in a non-traditional job agreement such as a shared-time or part-time plus commission structure. I have heard from many job seekers that salaries are not what they used to be, and if this is a concern for you, this is the chance for you to reinvent the salary game so you can create a company or job structure that allows you to earn more because you are giving up the so-called 'security' of a salaried position. If you have a sense that something else is available, consider this your opportunity to explore another route to replacing your income.

These are not all of the obstacles you might encounter; however, these are the most common I've seen. Above all, the #1 strategy all great sales people use is to NEVER GIVE UP! No matter what the obstacle you may be encountering, there is a way past it. You can: Get new information, create a new strategy, find additional resources or ask for help from someone else. If you commit to getting a job, you will get one!

The good news is that good companies are always hiring, and if you are talented, these good companies are looking for you!

Day 8 Recap

1. Rise at your regular workday time.
2. Shower, Shave & Starbucks.
3. Determine what's eating you? Anything at all?
4. Create a list of all you have accomplished since you were laid off. Celebrate your efforts.
5. What's next? Take a look at your list and determine who you will

contact next.

Day

9

Yes, You Can (They Did It; You Can Too)

If you are looking for inspiration, this is the place to find it. These are true stories from job seekers just like you. The message in each of these stories? Never, ever give up!

Down and Out But Showing UP Every Day

I met a young man I will call "Sam" one night when I went to speak at a local church career outreach meeting. Sam was young, perhaps 28 or 29 years old. He had a young family to support and desperately needed to find a job. He had done everything 'right' from filling out hundreds of applications to submitting as many resumes. And, yet a job eluded him.

I learned from the church's outreach coordinator that Sam, who usually had a great attitude had started to feel down about his situation. The coordinator felt he would benefit from having a 'task' to do, so she asked him if he would prepare an introduction for me, and asked him to meet with me prior to my speech that night.

Though his spirit was dampened by the lack of progress he was making in his job search, he put on a brave face each week and attended the meeting. In short, he kept showing up and moving.

When I arrived at the meeting, the church career outreach meeting coordinator made sure she was deliberately late so Sam and I would have time to chat. Her idea seemed to be working. When I arrived, Sam was full of a great attitude and happy to serve.

During that informal conversation, I could feel Sam's spirit lighten up as we talked and laughed. I asked him which company he would like to work for, and he (like many others) talked about the big companies that everyone seems to want to work with. When I asked what kind of work he was looking for, he went where many people go after some time 'on the market' that he would take 'any job,' but I wouldn't let him off the hook with such a generic answer. I asked him what he enjoyed in his past positions. After getting to know him and his specific experience, I thought of a client of mine that I felt he would be perfect for. I asked him if he would mind if I talked to my friend about an interview. He was excited about the opportunity.

When I arrived home that night, I sent a note to my friend and the next day, the company interviewed and hired him. A year or so later, that same company was purchased by a larger company and Sam benefitted from that sale, too. He is still working there.

This entire book is designed to prepare you for an opportunity just like this – where a person you don't yet know can help you connect to the job you need to get right *now*.

Lesson Learned: Keep showing up. Do what you know to do. Say yes, when asked to serve. Never, ever give up on yourself. Things can change overnight!

Changing your mind about what you think you really want

Because I have spoken to so many career outreach groups over the last decade and also people who have been in transition, I have had the fortunate opportunity to talk to many people who have a very different life today than they did even five years ago.

One such person is a man I'll call Greg who had spent two decades working in a Fortune 500 sales team. Greg told me about his job search and a turn it took that ended up giving a greater quality of life than he even knew existed in sales.

Like many people, Greg entered his job search on auto pilot looking for an identical replacement for the job he had lost. Same sized company (Fortune 500), same type of product, same environment he was used to – he simply figured that is what he knew and that is what he should continue doing.

It wasn't until fate stepped in and directed Greg to a *middle-market* company that he learned that there are many smaller companies that are strong, solid employers that offer many fringe benefits, including less travel, more quality of life and, most surprising, an even better benefits package!

Greg has been with his new employer for nearly three years now. He has spent more time with his family, his golf game has improved and he looks younger than he did 10 years ago.

Lesson Learned: Stay open to opportunities that don't look like what you think you want; it may bring you more than you expect. If you have been submitting your resume to a certain size company, ask what other company could benefit from your talents? Is it time to reconsider what you really want?

Focusing on what you do have and going for it

A woman who did not have a degree felt overwhelmed with the new job market. Listening to reports on the news and online about people with MBAs and Ph.D.s unable to secure jobs left her judging herself for not finishing her degree and demoralized about her chances of finding a job in an overcrowded job market.

Like many job seekers, she had abandoned her specific choice job for an 'any job will do' mentality. By submitting her resume to jobs far below her expertise, she did not receive any call backs. Demoralized, her hope began to vanish. She felt like there was no way she could compete in the competitive market when she did not have a degree. Like many people who begin to lose hope, she began to focus on what *she didn't have* instead of what she *did have*.

After one coaching session, she was able to articulate the ideal type of job that would excite her to go to each day. The more excited she became as she envisioned this ideal job, she began to remember the *passion* she brought to the table for her job. She realized that her *passion* was her greatest strength and her *enthusiasm* was her best-selling differentiator.

Armed with a renewed sense of confidence surrounding her abilities, her career experience and with her fears about not having a degree tucked safely behind her, she committed to her search again. However, she did not get far. *Without even sending out one more resume,* a recruiter who had reached out to her *13 months* prior to that time called her the *next day.* She had made a *lasting impression* on the recruiter and had a company she believed would be a perfect fit. She had a new job within a week.

Lesson Learned: Focus on what you do best, and do not compare yourself to others. Be clear about what your very best talent is. If your hope has dwindled, renew your hope by staying focused and re-committing to what you really want.

Give it all you've got

After 20 years in a job that would soon be ending, a woman I'll call Mary felt too old, too outdated and too ill-equipped to get the job she really wanted.

During a short conversation, Mary revealed that she secretly had been wanting to work for a prestigious university and had recently heard that her 'dream job' was about to be open. After sharing every excuse in the book about 'why' she couldn't have what she wanted, and after a few stern words about why *she had nothing to lose,* we worked on creating a new resume and a creative cover letter that could do the heavy lifting for her.

After a pep-talk and a boost from her new tools, Mary decided to give it a try. She mailed in the cover letter and resume with high hopes, but really didn't expect to get a call back. Instead, she continued to send out resumes to other positions that were more like the position she was leaving.

Three weeks went by and Mary had not even thought about the cover letter and resume she sent to her dream employer. That is, until she received a call from the administrator who *had to meet* the woman who wrote the cover letter Mary had sent in. It was her passion for fundraising that caught the administrator's attention. Her *creativity* shined above all the rest of the applicants, and Mary secured the job she had always secretly wanted.

Lesson Learned: While you are applying for jobs, why not apply for your 'dream job,' too? What do you have to lose? Creative cover letters stand out and can help you get your foot in the door. Use your own brand of creativity to get noticed. It's never too late to do what you might have done. Go for it!

Day 9 Recap

1. Shower, Shave & Starbucks.
2. Revisit your job seeking goals.
3. Visualize your ideal job.
4. Commit to your job quest.
5. Focus on what is *best* about you. Forget the rest.
6. Go for it!

Day

10

Frequently Asked Questions & Answers

I've spoken to thousands of people looking for a job over the last few years, and these top the frequently asked questions.

1. What do I do when I don't know what company I want to work for?

If you don't know what company you want to work for, how do you expect other people to help you? You must figure this out! So, begin by imagining it was a perfect world for a moment. What is the position you've imagined or always dreamed of working in or company you've wanted to go to work for? Then do some research on that company. It may be something you've always thought about but it may or may not be something that's really viable for you. You won't know until you research it!

With the internet today we have all kinds of opportunities at our doorsteps. Go online and look up the job that you do. Research companies that are similar to a company you've worked for where you've performed this job before. You will surely find many companies that you didn't even know about before.

Another thing to do if you don't know what company you want to work for is to talk with other people who know your business – people who do what you do. Ask them what other companies they know about to do the job or activities that you know how to do and then list those. Research those and see if those make sense for you.

Talk to people in your professional association that work for all different companies. Your professional association probably has chapters all over the United States where you can access people in other parts of the country to talk with, and see what companies there are that might be of interest for you.

First and foremost though….even if it is hard, you must figure out what companies you want to work for. I always recommend finding three companies that you want to go to work for so then you can share with others those three companies and then perhaps they can help you.

2. What do I do when I don't know anyone at the company I want to work for?

You need to talk to other people. Send out an email to everybody in your contact database and say, *"Hi, Does anyone know Company XYZ? I want to meet someone there and would appreciate an introduction to anyone you might know there."*

You can also look up the company online to see who is listed from the company. Perhaps, the management staff is listed on their website. Ask other people if they know any of these people. Use LinkedIn or other online resources to look up each of the people listed. Look for people that work for the company, too. See if you're connected to anyone at that company already.   Even if you are connected two or three people out it is still ok to ask for their introduction to who you want to know.

Remember the exercise the Rule of 250? Go back to your Rule of 250. Tell those 250 people which company you want to go to work for and see who knows somebody that they can introduce you to.

3. What do I do when I need help but I'm afraid to ask?

You know the Nike slogan? Just do it! You have got to get over this…the sooner the better! It is imperative that you ask other people to help you. I promise you they WANT to help you. Consider this: they just don't know what you need; otherwise they would have helped you already!

Finding a job is not a one-man sport. It is a team sport and there are many people that would love to be on your team to help you get a job *now*. Remember the Jerry McGuire movie a few years back? There was a line from the film, "Help me, help you!" Let others know *specifically* what you need help with and they will help you!

Everyone is uncomfortable at some time or another about asking for help. If you really are struggling with asking for help stop for a moment and think about someone you know. If they asked you for help would you be offended by that? Would you refuse to help them? Surely you wouldn't. You would help anyone if you knew what it was that they needed help with.

So this is one of those fears, the many fears, about finding a new job, but this being afraid to ask for help is one that you just simply have to work on and get over, just ask the question…TODAY!

4. What do I do when I need help but don't have any money?

In this day and time we are so lucky to have incredible resources at our finger tips via the internet. If you don't have money to get help there are plenty of resources you can access to get information at no charge. We have some of those listed in our reference guide here, but go online and research exactly what you are looking for and see what you come up with.

Think about the kind of help you need, put in the questions and see what comes up for you. There are plenty of free resources, plenty of online sources that answer questions that would be easy for you to find.

One other thing is to think about who might have the information that you need and perhaps you have information they need. You could barter and it won't cost either of you any money but both of you can share your expertise with one another and help move you along your job search path.

5. What do I do when things aren't moving?

When things aren't moving you really first need to ask yourself what you have been doing. Be honest with yourself. Have you followed all the suggestions here in the book? Do you have an action plan each day?

Generally what you'll find when things aren't moving is that you aren't moving. So you must look at what you're doing and think about what's one thing you could do today to move forward. Just one! That one thing could be to call somebody *today*, to email someone *today*, to talk to someone *today* or have a cup of coffee with someone *today* and share what you're working on, share what you're frustrated with, share what you need help with. Doing just one thing will generally get things moving quicker.

If this continues to be a struggle for you, then think about who can be a partner for you that can hold you accountable each day to what it is you say you want to do. Who can you trust that you could talk to each day and tell them what you will commit to do on that day and then the next day let them know you did it? Your check-in might sound like this, *"Yesterday I made five calls, I had two coffee appointments and I sent 13 emails, and I got one interview"* …whatever it is you committed to do. This might be something that you can do for someone else and they can do for you. It can be a win-win for both of you and keep you *both* moving so this process can work.

6. What do I do when people say they will help me and they don't call back?

Well, the truth is they do want to help you, but, like you, they get busy… they forget. Your situation doesn't impact them in the same way that it impacts you. So, you don't want to send any ill thoughts to them, but if they don't call back and you really think they have information then there's no problem with calling them again to say, *"Hi, Have you had time to talk to… or do… whatever it is that they committed to?"* The truth is, just like you, people don't always remember or follow through.

Can you remember when you were employed a time when someone asked you to help them? Did you always follow up quickly? Did you treat it as an urgent matter? Probably not. How many people did you help find a job when you were employed with your job? The sad thing is that many people didn't do anything to help anyone else when they were employed, and so when they're now unemployed and perhaps desperate and in dire need of a job, they call people, people that care about them, and they think they're going to react quickly, but they don't necessarily do it. It's just about being human. It is not about not caring. Try not to get wrapped up in blame. It's *your* job to stay in action, and that includes following up with those who committed to help you!

7. What do I do when I know what to do but can't get myself to move to get started?

This could be various things. Part of it is probably being scared. Are you just scared to get started? You're paralyzed. If so, try to think of one thing you can do today. Who is *one* person that you can call. Who is *one* person you can send an email to?

If it is that you think it might be depression and you've never been depressed before, and you feel very down like you can't do anything, then get yourself to a doctor, to a professional, to a counselor. If, in fact, you can't afford these kind of things then in your community there are generally resources for those who can't afford to pay for them that you can utilize. Call your city offices and talk to them and they will surely be able to help you.

It is really important to be honest with yourself what you are and aren't doing so you can figure out how to get past it. Think about a time in your past where there was something you knew how to do but you just didn't do it. How did you move past that? What things did you do that helped get you moving again? Consider if those things might also work for this situation of finding a new job. Remember, though, that you must, *you must* get yourself started again.

It may be that you're still angry that you lost your job or were let go. In that case, you have to deal with this. Anger is one of the various steps of a grief process. Losing a job is a loss, and where there's loss, the grief process follows. Acknowledge that, let yourself feel angry, sad or whatever it is and know that it is a process so you can get through it more quickly.

Sometimes you just need to talk to someone else – to say things out loud. Or, you need to be acknowledged so you then you can move on. If it is that you just cannot deal with it right now then allow yourself to set your anger, sadness, fear aside. For today, you have got to move forward and find a new job.

8. What do I do when I really want to change careers or industries but

need to make what I used to make?

Do not think that because you're changing careers or industries that you're going to necessarily make less. The truth is you might make more. So, think about why you want to change and learn about the new industry or business. What are the job opportunities available there? What are the salary ranges there? How can you translate what you've done in the past into those new opportunities? You might be amazed at how much more you can do.

If it is something you are certain you want to do and there is a pay decrease, then think about other things that you can do to generate income while you are building up your new career.

Please Note: I do not usually recommend a total career change when you lose your job unless you have already been thinking about a different career or industry and have done your research and homework already.

9. What do I do when the new company I want to work for is in another town and I don't know anyone there?

The good news is today we have tools like LinkedIn. You've already done your Rule of 250 exercise. Stop for a moment and think about yourself. Are the only people you know just the people in the town where you live now? Surely not.

You know people who live everywhere and so you need to reach out to *everyone* you know!

If you, for example, want to go to San Francisco for an opportunity there, then don't think about only being able to reach out to people in San Francisco. Go back to your list from Rule of 250 and reach out to *all* of them and ask them. If you don't know anyone in San Francisco, who do *they* know in San Francisco? If you want to work at a specific company that you can name in San Francisco, then go to your LinkedIn, go to your Facebook, and see who else works in San Francisco…who else lives in San Francisco that you could reach out to and ask them about the company that you're interested in. It is no longer difficult to be able to reach someone in another town, even though you don't live there.

So, think about yourself. Say, perhaps, you know someone in New York. Wouldn't you be willing to introduce them to your friend that wanted to go to New York? Well, of course you would. So this is an easy one.

Also, one of the things when you plan to move to a new town, whether you're doing it to be closer to family or you just want to live in a different part of the country, you do need to think about moving expenses and those kind of things in case the new company isn't willing to relocate you. Is this job in the new town attractive enough to you to take on added expenses? Or, can you make enough money to cover your moving expenses and other expenses that it takes to move from one place to another? Don't forget to think about ALL the things associated with a move.

10. What do I do when I don't get called back?

Have you sent a thank you note? Have you followed up with the different people that you interviewed with? Sometimes when you go to interview with a company you have to interview with two or three different people. Did you go after this job through an HR department or through an executive search firm? If so, go back to that person and let him or her know that you really want to know the status of the job you've interviewed for. Sometimes people don't want to know why they didn't get a position, but the truth is you do want to know because the quicker you understand *why* you didn't get the position, then the better you're going to be able to do on the *next* opportunity. Sometimes the reason you didn't get a call back is they decided not to add that position or they had other candidates internally so they're not going outside the company or they hired someone else for the position. There could be a myriad of reasons that they don't call back, so just keep trying.

11. What do I do when I'm getting interviews but I always come in second or third in the hiring process?

In a way, this is good news! You are getting interviews so you have obviously successfully figured out the part of the equation that gets you an interview, so that's great! And, if you're coming in second or third and, though you are not getting you a paycheck, it is still good news that you are interviewing well.

Go back and talk to the hiring company or recruiter. Don't say anything about the person they hired. Acknowledge that you know they've selected another candidate and, in order for you to improve yourself, you're wondering if they might give you feedback on what else you might have done to get this position. Be humble. Be earnest. The feedback may come in the form of maybe you didn't have a particular skill or accreditation, it may be that you didn't have as many years of experience, or it might be something else that just wasn't a good fit with that company. You need to know whatever it is. So, just call back and ask them.
Always do it with the attitude of wanting to understand and wanting to be the best you can be. You are not calling back to challenge them about the decision or who it is they did hire.

Day 10 Recap

1. Shower, Shave & Starbucks.
2. Be honest. Do any of these questions reflect where you are now?
3. Address any current concerns.
4. Commit to your job quest.
5. Design your day for tomorrow.
6. Go for it!

Resources

These resources will help you with the steps outlined in this book. This is not meant to be an exhaustive resource list; however, these are meant to help you quickly access what you need so you can stay in action. Please do your best to get your tools ready, and be aware that too much reading or searching for information will take you away from the daily actions that *will* help you get a job *now*.

See <u>VIRTUAL APPENDIX</u> for resources.

Web Resources

Nearly every company that you could want to work for will be listed on the Internet. A simple Google search will yield these web sites. If you aren't sure which companies you want to work for, then search the industry in which you want to work. See which companies come up first. Look around the site. What do their press releases say they are doing? What does their careers section say? Do you feel drawn to the company?

If you are looking for the companies that are the "Best Places to Work" then do a search for that term to get a national list, and then also do a search with your city's name *with* 'Best Places to Work' to get a local list. Remember that Fortune 500 is not the only show in town. Many mid-sized businesses are thriving, and you can find them by searching for local business awards in your area. Also, consider looking up the local business paper in your area – a *Business Journal* or a *Crain's* will provide a listing of companies in nearly every industry.

With many people moving in and out of jobs these days, you might find it a little harder to locate former colleagues. LinkedIn and Facebook can help you get in touch with people who have relocated.

Research is like being a detective. Part of harnessing the power of the web is knowing what to look for in the first place!

Traditional Resources

Remember to access 'traditional' resources that are oldies but goodies. Your local paper's career section may have employer spotlights, for example. The library is a wealth of information – for free. When you talk to librarians, they may also direct you to new books that have just arrived that may provide more up-to-date information for resume writing or keywords for your resume.

Try to look at traditional references as 'new' again. They may seem new to you if you haven't used them in quite some time!

www.ingramcontent.com/pod-product-compliance
Lightning Source LLC
Chambersburg PA
CBHW030406160726
47992CB00007B/2986